Growth Thinking

also by Nader Sabry

Ready Set Growth Hack:
A beginners guide to growth hack success

Growth Thinking

think, design, growth hack - a design
approaching to growth hacking

www.MyGrowthThinking.com

By Nader Sabry

Ordering information: Special discounts are available on quantity purchases by governments, NGOs, schools, companies, associations, and others. For details, contact the publisher at www.nadersabry.com.

Printed in the United States of America and Canada.

Nader Sabry, Growth Thinking: think, design, growth hack - a design approaching to growth hacking

Ebook	ISBN 978-1-9163569-4-8
Paperback	ISBN 978-1-9163569-5-5
Hardcover	ISBN 978-1-9163569-6-2
Audiobook	ISBN 978-1-9163569-7-9

1. BUSINESS & ECONOMICS / Entrepreneurship, 2. BUSINESS & ECONOMICS / Corporate Finance / Venture Capital, 3. BUSINESS & ECONOMICS / Industries / Computers & Information Technology

First Edition, and first print in 2020

Nader Sabry
Royal Oak. P.O. Box 91022
Calgary Alberta, Canada T3G 0B1

www.nadersabry.com

GET A COPY

Bestselling book Ready, Set, Growth hack for more insights into the growth hacking blueprint…

"HE IS THE GUY YOU DON'T WANT YOUR COMPETITION TO HIRE..."

NADER SABRY

READY
SET
GROWTH
HACK

88
GROWTH HACKING
TOOLS TO GET
YOU STARTED

A BEGINNER'S GUIDE TO
GROWTH HACKING SUCCESS

https://www.amazon.com/Ready-Set-Growth-hack-beginners/dp/1916356915

SCAN & START NOW

Quickly learn how to use the Growth thinking methodology **like a Ninja**

+ **$99 hacking** growth thinking designs training **course FREE**

+ **$199 10 secrets** of Growth Thinking training **course FREE**

CONTENTS

INDEX

Index all 20 of your growth hacks her by name

1. Name of hack
2. Name of hack
3. Name of hack
4. Name of hack
5. Name of hack
6. Name of hack
7. Name of hack
8. Name of hack
9. Name of hack
10. Name of hack
11. Name of hack
12. Name of hack
13. Name of hack
14. Name of hack
15. Name of hack
16. Name of hack
17. Name of hack
18. Name of hack
19. Name of hack
20. Name of hack

INTRODUCTION

Growth thinking explained

INTRODUCTION

Growth thinking is a fast, easy, and simple way to prototype growth hacks. This enables growth by visualizing a growth hack in abstract and then detailing them into a systematic approach. This makes it easy to develop and improve growth hacks and generate new, better growth hacks.

For freestyle thinking to occur, it's essential to have a method that allows our creativity to thrive. Growth thinking is all about the processes on how that takes place. It's a methodology design to help you get your mind wrapped around growth hacking. But it goes beyond this; it's a structured process where you can look at all aspects of what is involved from costs, measures ROI, and learning's that transform into new growth hacks.

This progressive process allows you to capture your thinking and work with others to get feedback like a prototype. As a prototype, you're back to thinking through what will work, what may not work, what else can be done, and what will be involved to make this growth hack work.

Growth hackers have designed this method with the growth hacking process in mind. One of the challenges with the growth hacking field is it's an emerging discipline where many practices have not been standardized yet.

The benefits of growth thinking by:

From idea to action - accurately and rapidly turn growth hacking ideas into execution quickly and cost-effectively,

Think at scale - quickly and effortlessly find methods to take an abstract growth hack, structure it and scale it, and

Save time and money - rapidly prototype your growth hacking ideas saving time and money.

..and these benefits happen because of:

Visualization - design thinking approach to quickly and easily see how a growth hack will work,

Systemize - Turn designs into structured sequences that turn an idea into an actual growth hack,

Optimization - instantly find improvements and generate new better growth hacks with little effort,

Rapid development - the systematic learning approach accelerates the improvement and development of new growth hacks, and

Collaboration - swiftly and efficiently get feedback and co-create growth hacks with others

What is growth hacking

The biggest testament to growth hacking is unicorns (billion dollar startup companies) as this is their secret weapon. This is when a small never heard about startup company disrupt a space they dominate and control by significantly shifting everything. Those new rules are defined and pushed by growth hackers who leverage that for their own gains.

A straightforward and powerful way of understanding growth hacking is about getting disproportionate results—fewer inputs, for a much more significant outcome. The transition point in the middle is where a growth hacker does his/her magic by using fewer resources to generate a disproportionate result with a massive ROI (return on investment).

GROWTH HACKING SUCCESS FORMULA

(mindset+ process) x (culture + strategy) x (talent + technology)

Although we get caught-up on tech, without the right mindset and process to drive it, then culture and strategy cannot form a direction, let alone align the right talent and technology to grow..

This is defined by a growth hacking mindset that endorses a culture of being lean, quick, and very tech-oriented. Although tech plays a significant part, this doesn't mean you have to be a tech business, as many past cases have proven even traditional business models tap into growth hacking, including companies like McDonald's.

Why growth thinking

Growth thinking is a design system that helps growth hackers visualize and evaluate their growth hacks. This enables you to answer questions like:

> How to design a growth hack
>
> How to improve the design of growth hack
>
> How to execute the growth hack
>
> How to improve the growth hack
>
> How to scale the growth hack
>
> How to monetize the growth hack

This systematic design method allows growth hackers to think structurally but in a creative way. This will enable you to test, evaluate, and improve growth hacks quickly, efficiently, and at a low cost. This allows growth hackers to share their designs with other growth hackers who can help improve and take their growth hacks to the next level.

The collection of growth hacks becomes your playbook; growth hackers can keep track of their progress. This design system approach lets growth hackers detect significant learnings and generate new, more powerful growth hacking ideas. Over the course of the 20 growth hacks, this will become your playbook that you use to grow.

Methodology

This design method uses a five-part process; profiling, designing, sequencing, testing, and learning's. The methodology works like this. You have a spark of an idea for a growth hack; you jump straight into prototyping blank pages using a growth hacking design language. This design language uses nine symbols to map out the design and systematically structure it from an idea to action. Once you're done, profile it, then sequence the growth hack with the details to execute it. Then put it to the test, and learn from it. The learning transforms into successes you scale or failures that generate new hacks.

This progressive process helps you develop a solid playbook to be used for exponential growth. The learning process, which is in three layers, helps accelerate this. The first layer is learning per each growth hack, the second is learning from every five growth hacks, and the third is learning from all 20 growth hacks. This is achieved by identifying patterns that help, improve, or create better growth hacks..

The growth hacking design language is made-up of these elements.

1. Process

2. Decision

3. Input

4. Output

5. Flow

6. Integration

7. Repeat

8. Limitations

9. Stop

Let's take a closer look into this. It's important to understand this simple system as what you will be practicing per hack. This system draws on workflow processing and growth hacking fundamentals into a single symbolic system.

introduction

▭	Process	→	Flow
◇	Decision	⇄	Integration
→	Input	↻	Repeat
←	Output	≡	Limitations
		STOP	Stop

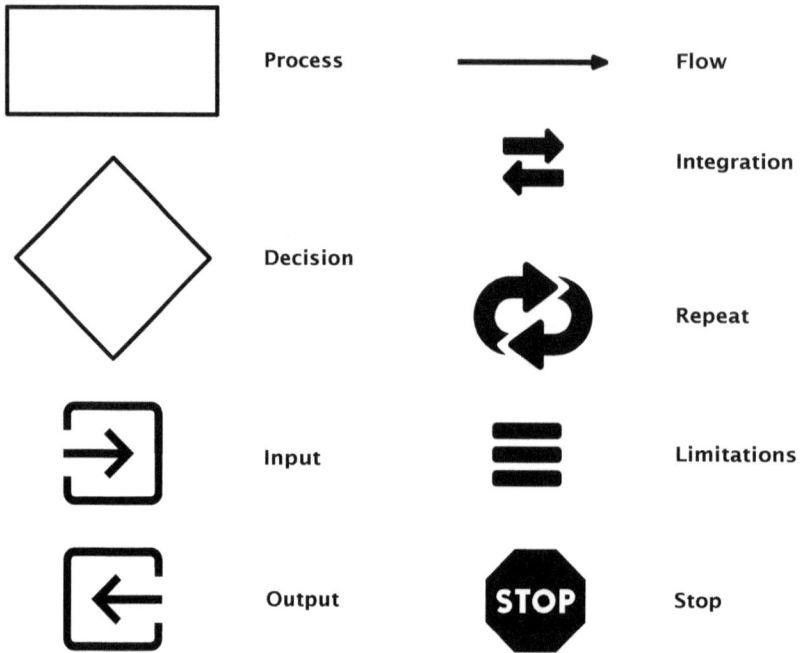

This symbol-based system enables you to wireframe your growth hack design instantly. This freestyle approach allows you to get your growth hack working quickly to evaluate what would be needed to make this happen.

This helps you with:

What does this hack look like? - this allows you to visualize the hack from start to end,

What is involved? - this will enable you to see all details from a top-level design,

How to make it work? - this will allow you to see how everything connects visually,

How did it perform? - this will enable you to see what parts worked and what did not work, and

Improvements to make it better? this allows you to generate new hacks from successes and failures

The process is a creative yet structured approach to growth hacking. The sequencing part is a log of the drawings in the prototype where you would state the specific details related to those parts of the growth hack like data to be used, sources to draw on, tools to utilize, people who will be involved, etc... This is powerful because it allows you to see a top-level visual summary backed with details to develop the growth hack instantly.

Science behind the design system

This process blends into five different methods into a single process. This all originates from the blueprint developed in "Ready Set Growth Hack, A beginners guide to growth hacking success," The five methods used are:

- Growth hacking cycle,
- Workflow,
- Design thinking,
- FPL (fail, pass, learn) system, and
- Playbook development

The Growth hacking cycle is based on defining growth problems, growth hacking it, and scaling it. The workflow method is a symbol-based system for process design. Design thinking is a visualized approach to integrating many different parts for developing a solution. The FPL system is a development methodology for growth hacks to improve, optimize, and generate new growth hacks.

Finally, playbook development is a journaling system approach where different ideas are documented and tested and eventually evolve into final strategies.

Growth cycle

A growth cycle is a three-phase approach starting with growth problems, growth hacking, and growth extensions. This cycle is a dynamic approach to building exponential, scalable, and long-term sustainable growth.

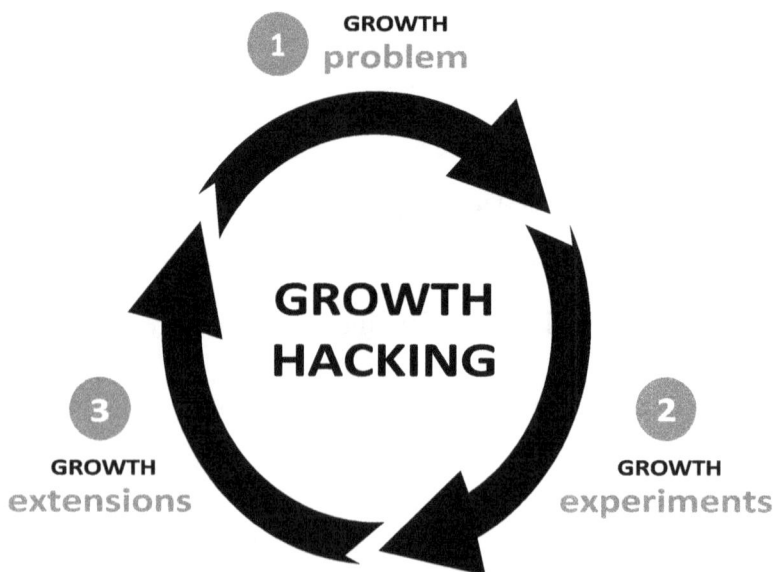

The growth problem is defining and structuring the growth problem and pinpointing where to start and grow. The growth experiment is the growth hacking process. This is driven by a structured experimentation process that allows the best growth hacks to emerge. Once the best appear, further development takes place to scale the hack and develop enhancements and new hacks based on those hacks. Growth extensions are about converting scalable growth hacks into full-scale operations, ensuring automation and structured and integrated processes support the long-term sustainable growth of the growth hacks.

Workflow

Workflows originate in manufacturing traced to Frederick Taylor and Henry Gantt. A workflow is a systematic approach to organizing activities in an optimal format. This is achieved by visually understanding sequences, hierarchy, and other relationships that would have usually been challenging to establish quickly and easily. This is the basis of optimizing processes that enable automation and scalability.

The underlying drafting system, which is how processes are used in growth thinking to use standard symbols, illustrates the process and relationship of working parts in a growth hack. Workflow has become central to scaling and automation for almost every industry on the planet today.

Design thinking

Design thinking is a prototyping process that entails context analysis, problem-finding/framing, ideation-solution generating, creative thinking, sketching and drawing, modeling and prototyping, testing, and evaluating. Design thinking's primary purpose is to manage poorly defined problems and abstract situations via a solution-based modeling process.

This is applied in growth thinking, but quickly and easily prototyping a growth hack, visually allowing abstract concepts to exist, but yet to be defined and further structured intuitively.

FPL System (Fail, Pass, Learn)

The FPL system (fail, pass, learn) is a dynamic and objective approach that accelerates experiments through progressive learning. This advanced learning allows experiments to develop into a sustainable system, where a pass or fail can be transformed into knowledge and then into ideas that feed new experiments.

This feed of new experiments allows growth hackers to focus by drawing on resources and capabilities already used without letting them go to waste. This process provides a platform for growth hackers to see meta-patterns. For example, a series of experiments may be failing but collectively have an extremely high learning value that can lead to significant growth.

Failures are constructive because they give clues about what not to do and changes that might reverse the final results, leading to a pass and improved outcomes.

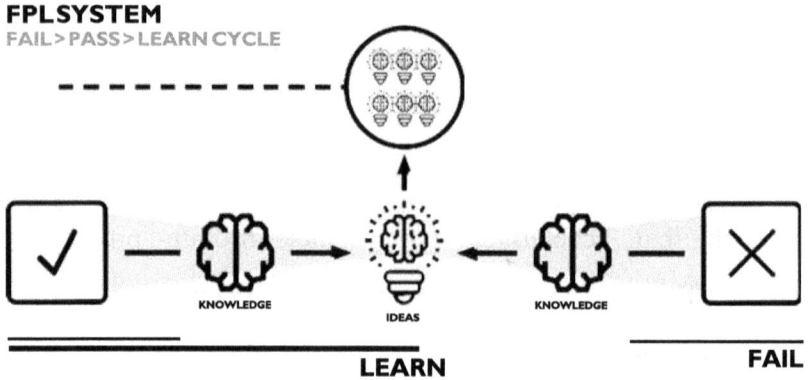

FPL SYSTEM
FAIL > PASS > LEARN CYCLE

KNOWLEDGE   IDEAS   KNOWLEDGE

LEARN   **FAIL**

The FPL system leads to 12 possible outcomes and the decision points that go with them.

FAIL OUTCOMES

1. FAIL: Complete failure discard

When an experiment is completely unstable, adjustable, or cannot be improved at all.

2. FAIL: Adjustments to pass

When an experiment has potential, but requires adjustments to improve outcomes

3. FAIL: New idea to pass

When an experiment has potential, but requires a whole new approach to retest.

PASS OUTCOMES

4. PASS: Complete pass; go to scale

When an experiment is a success and can go straight to scaling.

5. PASS: Improve it to make better

When an experiment is a success, but can use an effective improvement within it.

6. PASS: Add on to it to make better

When an experiment is a success, something can be added to make it even better.

LEARNING OUTCOMES

7. LEARN – FAIL: Why it didn't work and what to avoid

When an experiment fails, finding causes that led to failure, and determining how to not repeat them again in future experiments.

8. LEARN – FAIL: Why it didn't work and how it can be changed

When an experiment fails, finding causes that led to failure and how small adjustments could improve future experiments.

9. LEARN – FAIL: Why it didn't work, but a new better idea

When an experiment fails, finding causes that led to failure, but a new idea emerges as a solution to be used in future experiments.

10. LEARN – PASS: Next is bigger, better ideas to test from the start

When an experiment passes and several new and better direct or indirect ideas are generated for future experiments.

11. LEARN – PASS: Changes or improvements for next level

When an experiment passes, and adjusts and improvements can lead to even more successful experiments in the future.

12. LEARN – PASS: What elements can be reused in other ideas

When an experiment passes, specific elements that led to success can be reused in other ways in future experiments.

Playbook development

A playbook is a log of strategies that start in abstract and then implemented, improved, and finally logged as a play. The idea of a playbook originates from professional sports where coaches would visualize their on-field strategies, optimize them once implemented, and ultimately turn them into fundamental plays. They would eventually form their methodology for their team.

In growth thinking, it does precisely that through the learning process. The plays are combined into unique knowledge to enhance your thinking and implementation progressively. The winning plays become part of your growth strategy, and they consistently deliver winning results.

HOW TO DO THIS

Growth thinking is a five-step process that allows growth hackers to quickly, easily, and for a very low cost, visualize their growth hacks before implementing them. The five steps are:

1. **Profiling** - name, description, costs, ROI, and timing
2. **Designing** - designing the growth hack in a workflow format
3. **Sequencing** - detailing the design giving attributes to each element
4. **Testing** - fail, pass learning system to improve and generate new hacks
5. **Learning** - extracting learning's from several hacks to improve and develop new ones

Pen to paper, you start with design. The design process is based on a workflow design system with ten symbols. This symbol based system allows you to quickly wireframe your thinking, then detail it in the sequencing process. Once complete, you can complete its profile, run the tests, and extract the learnings.

You can start with a design because it allows your creativity to move quickly, but that doesn't mean you cannot begin profiling. Hence, you can either put some profile elements like the name and description and come back and fill out the rest later.

The five-step process is an intuitive process designed to unleash your creativity yet give structure without the process being over structure.

Step 1: Profile -

name, description, costs, ROI and timing

This step is about defining the growth hack, remember you do not have to detail all this to start with as you may want to start designing and come back here to finish off the profile.

1. Give your hack a **name**

   (e.g., diaper finder)
2. Give a brief **description** of the hack

   (e.g., Get best diapers at the best price for mothers)
3. Define the **growth problem** the hack is resolving

   (e.g., mothers don't know where to find the best diapers at the best price)

4. Define the target **Results** *(e.g., sell diapers)*
5. Define the **Measure** to get those results

   (e.g., sell 120k diapers this year)
6. Determine the **costs** for undertaking this hack *(e.g., $1000)*
7. Set a target **ROI (return on investment)** *(e.g. 10x = $10k)*

8. Who is the **Customer** (e.g., Mothers)

9. Who will be the **User** (e.g., babies)

10. Who are **Middlemen** involved (e.g., baby shops)

11. **Mindset** - What knowledge do you need to obtain?
    (e.g. HTML coding)

12. **Skillset** - how will you use that knowledge?
    (e.g., How to build a website)

13. **Toolset** - what tools do you need to use the knowledge obtained *(e.g., WordPress, Photoshop, Hosting provider, etc.)*

name	**Diaper empire**	1

description

Short and simple description of the growth hack

Use social media as a tool to educate and sell to mothers on how to get cheaper, better quality diapers easily online without having to think or do much — 2

problem

Short and specific description of the growth problem your solving

Mothers have trouble getting the best quality diapers for the best prices especially new-mothers as they are overwhelmed with all other other challenges – develop a tool that enables mothers to quickly and easily get good quality diapers for a good price — 3

results 4	measure 5	costs 6	ROI 7
10K diapers per month	*Diapers sold*	*$1,000*	*10x = 10K diapers*
(#) %	(#) %	(low) mid high	low (mid) high

timeframe 8

15 min	30 min	1 hour	1 day	2 days	3 days	4 days	5 days	7 days	10 days

Other time *30 days (September 2021)*

| **customer** | *Mothers – new mothers / small family* | **9** |
| Who will by paying for this | *mothers / Single mothers* | |

| **user** | *Babies* | **10** |
| Who will be consuming this | | |

| **middlemen** | *Online social media influencers* | **11** |
| Who is in the middle and why | *who target mothers* | |

mindset		*Social media marketing*	**12**
		Design for social media	
needed to solve this sort of problem and how to go about it		*Outreach on social media*	

skillset		*Content strategy and development*	**13**
		Graphic design	
specifically to execute this growth hack		*Outreach copy/strategy*	

toolset		*Buffer*	**14**
		Content Studio	
needed for execute this		*Grammarly*	
		Photoshop	
		Canva	

Step 2: Design -

designing the growth hack in a workflow format

Start drafting your ideas into a workflow using the symbol system to illustrate your growth hack. Let it flow without overthinking -- illustrate at a high level that captures all major parts involved.

1. Have starting **input**

   (e.g., find mother/baby forums and portals)

2. Draw the **processes** from start to finish using the symbols using the growth hacking design language

   (e.g., the process of how to find, qualify and reach mothers)

3. Have an end **output**

   (e.g., outreach emails to mothers)

☐	Process	→	Flow
◇	Decision	⇄	Integration
→	Input	↻	Repeat
←	Output	≡	Limitations
		STOP	Stop

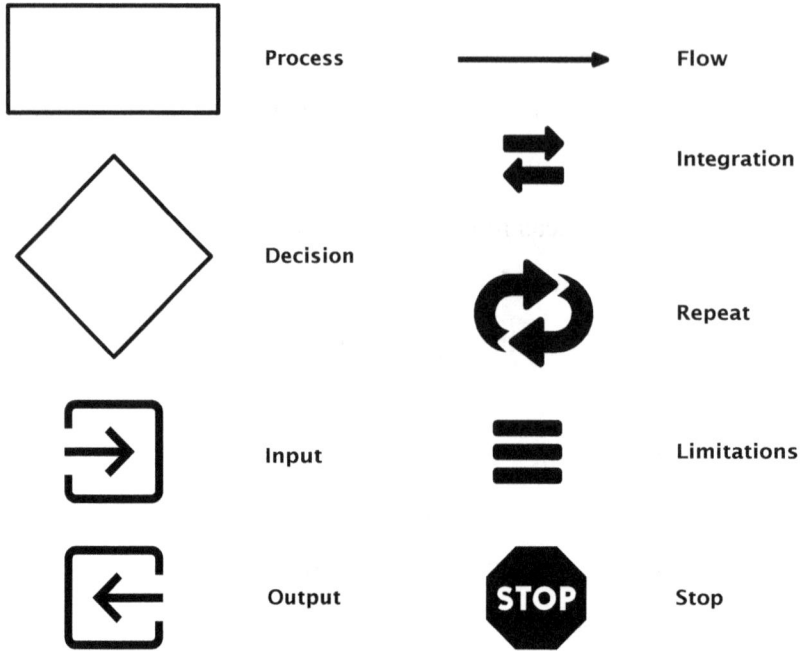

This is a very simple and straightforward symbol-based system and they can be briefly detailed with titles or headlines for each process. Save the details for the next step

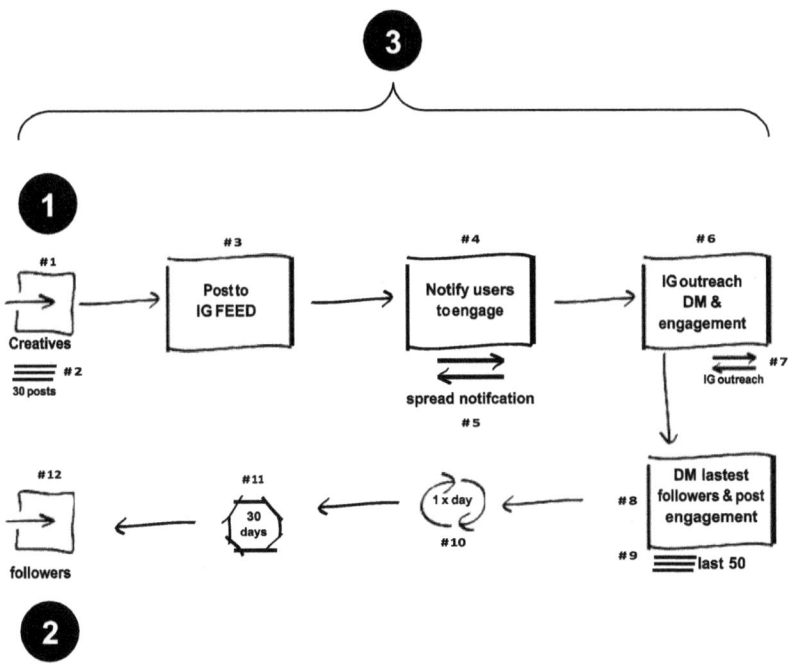

Step 3: Sequencing -

detailing the design giving attributes to each element

Sequencing is about getting the right details in a place like, data, sources, tools, and anything else specific to that part of the process for it to be executed.

1. **Sequence** each step in the drawing in chronological order
2. Create a **reference** number in your notes
3. **Detail the notes** in chronological order with specifications

The details are used to help ensure you covered everything possible, improve the process, and eventually develop it yourself or pass this on to someone else to create, whether in whole or in parts. This also stimulates collaboration by giving feedback and improvements to make adjustments.

3

1 - Creatives; *Daily focused quotes with inspiring images for*

inspiring mothers to get better quality diapers for their babies for a better

price – 150 word caption with 30 hashtags trending for mother and baby

related topics + mention 5 mother influencers

2 - Liitatioms; *Create 30 Instagram posts as 1080 x 1080*

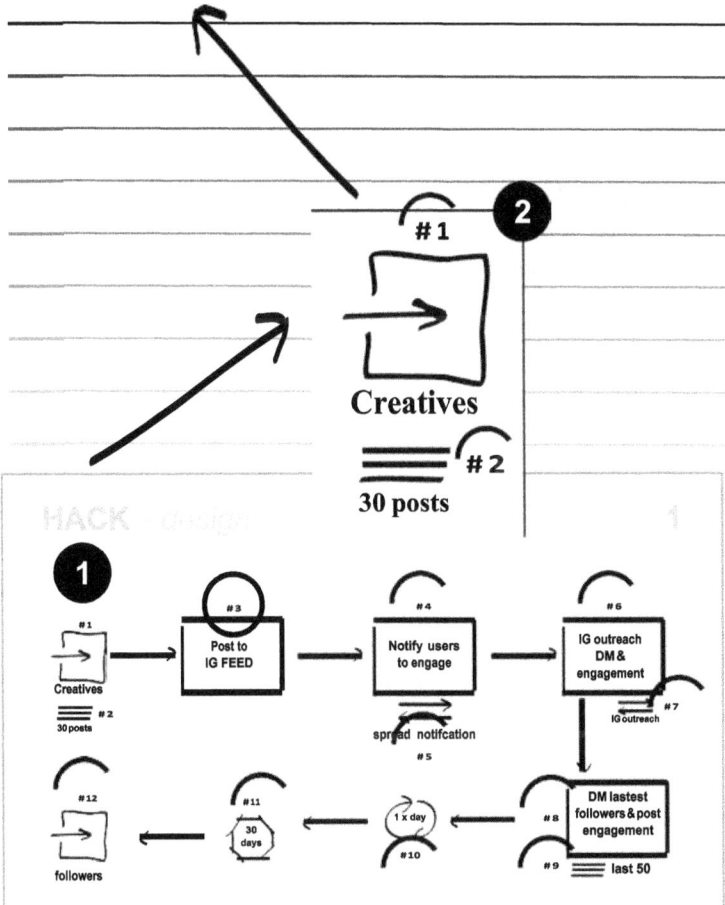

#1   **2**

Creatives

#2

30 posts

1

| #1 Creatives #2 30 posts | → | #3 Post to IG FEED | → | #4 Notify users to engage | → | #6 IG outreach DM & engagement |

spread notifcation #5

#7 IG outreach

#12 followers | ← | #11 30 days | ← | #10 1 x day | ← | #8 DM lastest followers & post engagement |

#9 last 50

HACK - design

Step 4: Test -

fail, pass learning system to improve and generate new hacks

Give the growth hack a try multiple times if needed to determine if the hack is a pass or fail. Once determined as a fail or pass, the outcomes are valuable in taking the next steps.

1. Check off **fail or pass**?
   (P1, P2, P3, F1 F2 or F3)
2. Select which the **outcome** of the hack
   (P4, P5 P6, F4, F5, or F6)
3. Write down the **learning's**

The learning's have two primary purposes, the first is to find improvements, and the second is to find new and better hacks stimulated from a pass or even failure of the growth hack. Take your time to reflect, even if this takes some time, and share this with others to get feedback.

1	**pass** ✓		☐ fail	
Complete pass go to scale	P1	F1	Complete failure **discard**
Improve it to make better	✓	F2	**Modifications** to pass
Add on to it to make better	P3	F3	**New** idea to pass

2	learning outcome - pass		fail - learning outcome	
Next bigger, better ideas to test from the start	✓	F4	Why didn't it work, and what to avoid
Changes or improvements for next level	P5	F5	Why didn't it work, but can be changed
What elements can be reused into other ideas	P6	F6	Why didn't it work, but a new better idea

3 learning | **What did you learn from whether a pass or a failure**
use the letter code and number your learning's

Mothers are the best people to sell to other mothers as they can

relate to each other and have deeper meaningful conversations

*hence its best to develop a network of **affiliates who are***

mothers to sell to other mothers

Step 5: Learning's -

extracting learning's from several hacks to improve and generate new ones

Learning isn't about success exclusively but also failures. Both have valuable outcomes that allow us to find better and new ways to drive growth hacking.

1. List **common** patterns and write them down
2. List ways to **improve** a success or a failing hack
3. List ways to **generate new growth hacks**

Keep in mind learning happens at three levels designed to accumulate your learning's into consolidated outcomes to pursue improvements or new growth hacks. The three levels are:

a. Per hack - this happens all every hack

b. Every five hacks - we take the last five hacks and find patterns

c. All 20 hacks - we take the learning's from every five and consolidate them

1 *1 - Trust*; mothers only trust other mothers especially ones with multiple children and single mothers are seen as hero's

2 - Influence; mothers follower on average 4 influencers but overlay consumer on avenge 1 of the 4 as there main source of information

3 – Connecting; mothers seek to connect with experts to help give them advise on how to be a better mother as they are never satisfied with their mothering skills.

2 *1 – Influencers*; get as many influencers onboard as possible

2 – Channels; use as many possible channels like other social media platforms and integrate the campaigns run

3 – Events; Run frequent online events to get more mothers into the funnel

3 *1 – affiliates*; develop a mothers sales affiliate network

2 – viral-loops; create viral-loop giveaways with brands they want

3 – Webinars; Create regular educational webinars at the to of the funnel

This is a progress bar representing, *each single* growth hack, then every *five combined* and collectively all *20 growth hacks*.

GROWTH HACKER MINDSET

Four main taxonomies determine a growth hacker's mind: drivers reach, decisions, and tools. The combination of the four forms the underlying idea of aching disproportionate results

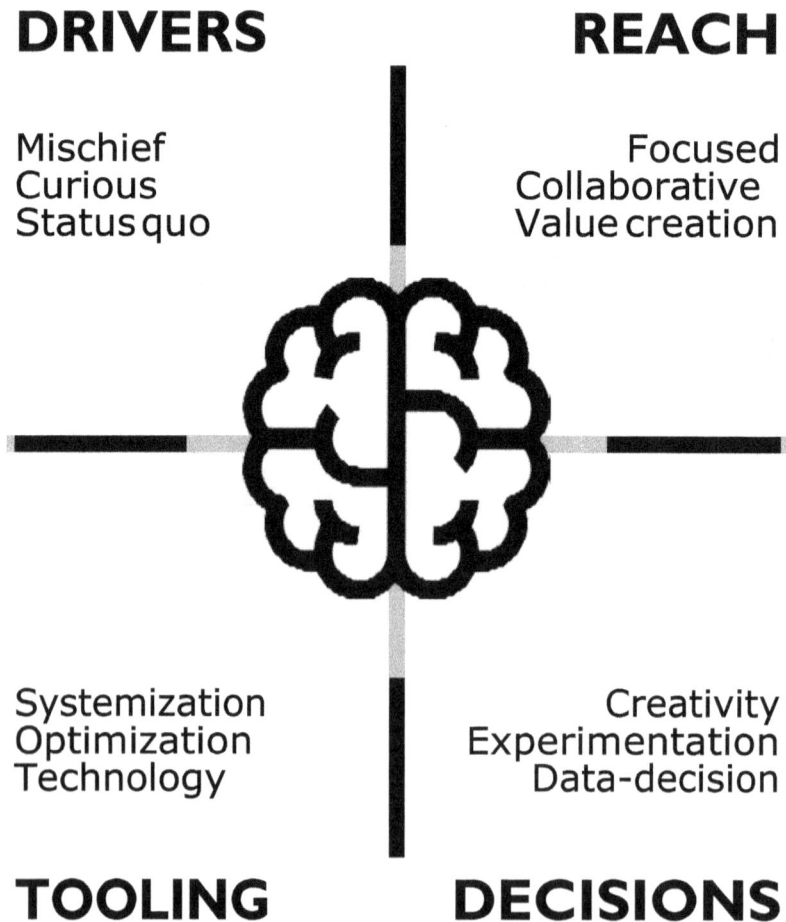

DRIVERS

Mischief
Curious
Status quo

REACH

Focused
Collaborative
Value creation

TOOLING

Systemization
Optimization
Technology

DECISIONS

Creativity
Experimentation
Data-decision

1. Drivers --

The drivers are the underlying motivations and stimuli that inspire how growth hackers think and take action.

Mischiefness

They deeply need to break the rules, as they do not believe in the rules they have not benefited from governing and limiting their way of life. Therefore this underpins their thinking to find a way to break the rules to their benefit.

Curiosity

They are fascinated by digging deeper into how things work by asking the big why questions. This allows them to better understand theories and phenomena to map out their mechanics to manipulate them toward their benefit.

.

Status quo

The general rules over institutionalization drive their need to challenge the establishments surrounding them. This allows them to break the rules and change the norms of how society around them works.

2. Reach --

Growth hackers have a goal to reach as many people as possible without the general population knowing how they did it.

Focused

They have an extremely focused approach by pinning done abstract problems and creating unique structures to solve them.

Collaborative

They have a resourceful approach where they work with like-minded people and find other cross-functional people to help reach their goals effectively.

Value-creation

They focus on creating value with monetization, often trying to reach the masses to make a change.

3. Decisions --

When hacking growth optimization is the goal to solve at a high-level, there is no one solution to a single problem but finding the fastest, easiest, and cheapest way.

Creativity

Growth hackers are resourceful; they find simple, fast, and digestible ways to solve problems. One of the challenges for growth hackers is thinking too technically.

Experimentation

They run tests and lots of them to determine the most optimal approach to getting results using all possible avenues.

Data-driven

They make decisions based on data, even if the data might potentially be blinding. Data helps determine the most optimal options.

4. Tools --

Growth hackers are always seeking new tools, optimizing existing ones, and finding optimal ways of connecting them to get solutions.

Systemization

For a solution to work, it needs to be automated, and when automated, the probability of scalability is a lot higher when seeking exponential growth.

Optimization

When finding the right tools and connecting them, the goals are optimizing the way they work together. This holistic approach helps maximize optimization.

Technology

Technology enables automation, scalability, and integration, which underpins growth even if you're a non-tech company.

The mindset of a growth hacker is defined by how he or she solves problems. The elements described above are the most common thinking patterns of growth hackers.

GROWTH HACKER HABITS

Growth hackers have 14 critical habits they work with. They do not work with all of them as a strength at once. You will find a single strength supported by three other habits and the rest for development over time. The 14 habits are:

1. Openness
2. Flexibility
3. No ego
4. Risk taking
5. Fresh perspective
6. Generosity
7. Curiosity

8. Team focused
9. Listen before action
10. Cohesive approach
11. Consensus
12. Diplomatic
13. Action driven
14. Collective win

1. Openness

They use an open approach to gain resources, using them, and find solutions to growth problems. This often is the underpinning factor behind their creativity.

2. Flexibility

When using an open approach, they work flexibly to solve growth problems knowing they don't have the exact solution but need to be flexible in finding it.

3. No ego

They focus on removing their ego from the equation; often, this is challenged by technical thinking - blinding them in finding creative solutions.

4. Risk-taking

They take bold yet calculated risks, often in a progressive manner, to manage unknown facts that are not seen early on.

5. Fresh perspective

They focus on finding new ways to solve existing problems by finding new solutions not yet attempted or poorly execute.

6. Generosity

They are open-handed to negotiate and broker the acquisition of new resources by being generous to open new doors.

7. Curiosity

They look deep into the whys. This helps them find unseen possibilities not seen by asking excellent questions and often challenging the status quo.

8. Team focused

They often are challenged with trust, but when they develop their small groups of trusted people, they thrive by forming collective learning and efforts.

9. Listen before action

They focus on getting good quality information before taking action to manage their risks and come up with better growth hacks quicker and easier.

10. Cohesive approach

They focus on developing networks beyond their teams for the exchange of know-how and cross development opportunities.

11. Consensus

They focus on developing a common approach to ensure buy-in and momentum to generate the energy needed to undertake large initiatives.

12. Diplomatic

They often are challenged with being diplomatic, which is key to ensuring relationships supersede technical barriers to get solutions.

13. Action driven

All their know-how and tools are geared towards taking action, leaving little space for theories that waste time and not get results.

14. Collective wins

Finding ways that everyone wins in the process, including those directly involved even if their role is minor in the overall outcome.

These *14 habits are specific* to growth hackers; they often draw on these habits as *their core capability*. With the focus on a *single superpower* among these habits, growth hackers *must develop their habits*.

HACK

Lets get designing those
growth hacks

name	

description

Short and simple description of the growth hack

problem

Short and specific description of the growth problem your solving

results	measure	costs	ROI
# %	# %	low mid high	low mid high

timeframe

15 min	30 min	1 hour	1 day	2 days	3 days	4 days	5 days	7 days	10 days

Other time

1   **HACK** - *profile*

customer

Who will by
paying for this

user

Who will be
consuming this

middlemen

Who is in the
middle and why

mindset

Knowledge
needed to solve
this sort of
problem and how
to go about it

skillset

The skills needed
specifically to
execute this
growth hack

toolset

List all tools
needed   for
execute this
growth hack

HACK – *sequencing*

1

sequence	**Data / tools / conditions / sources / techniques / process** *Use the sequence numbers in your drawings as references below*

_____

_____

_____

_____

_____

_____

_____

_____

_____

_____

_____

_____

_____

_____

_____

1   **HACK** – *sequencing*

pass				fail
Complete pass go to scale	P1		F1	Complete failure **discard**
Improve it to make better	P2		F2	**Modifications** to pass
Add on to it to make better	P3		F3	**New** idea to pass

learning outcome - pass				fail - learning outcome
Next bigger, better ideas to test from the start	P4		F4	Why didn't it work, and what to avoid
Changes or improvements for next level	P5		F5	Why didn't it work, but can be changed
What elements can be reused into other ideas	P6		F6	Why didn't it work, but a new better idea

learning	**What did you learn from whether a pass or a failure** *use the letter code and number your learning's*

_____

_____

_____

_____

_____

_____

_____

_____

_____

_____

_____

_____

_____

_____

_____

_____

_____

_____

_____

_____

_____

_____

_____

HACK – *profile*

name	

description

Short and simple description of the growth hack

problem

Short and specific description of the growth problem your solving

results	measure	costs	ROI
# %	# %	low mid high	low mid high

timeframe

15 min	30 min	1 hour	1 day	2 days	3 days	4 days	5 days	7 days	10 days

Other time

customer

Who will by
paying for this

user

Who will be
consuming this

middlemen

Who is in the
middle and why

mindset

Knowledge
needed to solve
this sort of
problem and how
to go about it

skillset

The skills needed
specifically to
execute this
growth hack

toolset

List all tools
needed for
execute this
growth hack

sequence	**Data / tools / conditions / sources / techniques / process**
	Use the sequence numbers in your drawings as references below

_____

_____

_____

_____

_____

_____

_____

_____

_____

_____

_____

_____

_____

_____

_____

_____

2   **HACK** – *sequencing*

—
—
—
—
—
—
—
—
—
—
—
—
—
—
—

	pass			fail	
Complete pass go to scale		P1	F1		Complete failure **discard**
Improve it to make better		P2	F2		**Modifications** to pass
Add on to it to make better		P3	F3		**New** idea to pass

learning outcome - pass			fail - learning outcome	
Next bigger, better ideas to test from the start	P4	F4	Why didn't it work, and what to avoid
Changes or improvements for next level	P5	F5	Why didn't it work, but can be changed
What elements can be reused into other ideas	P6	F6	Why didn't it work, but a new better idea

learning	**What did you learn from whether a pass or a failure** *use the letter code and number your learning's*

_____

_____

_____

_____

_____

_____

name	

description	
Short and simple description of the growth hack	

problem	
Short and specific description of the growth problem your solving	

results		measure		costs			ROI		
#	%	#	%	low	mid	high	low	mid	high

timeframe

15 min	30 min	1 hour	1 day	2 days	3 days	4 days	5 days	7 days	10 days

Other time

customer

Who will by
paying for this

user

Who will be
consuming this

middlemen

Who is in the
middle and why

mindset

Knowledge
needed to solve
this sort of
problem and how
to go about it

skillset

The skills needed
specifically to
execute this
growth hack

toolset

List all tools
needed for
execute this
growth hack

HACK – *sequencing*

3

sequence	**Data / tools / conditions / sources / techniques / process** *Use the sequence numbers in your drawings as references below*

_____

_____

_____

_____

_____

_____

_____

_____

_____

_____

_____

_____

_____

_____

_____

HACK – *testing*   3

pass				fail
Complete pass go to scale	P1	F1		Complete failure **discard**
Improve it to make better	P2	F2		**Modifications** to pass
Add on to it to make better	P3	F3		**New** idea to pass

learning outcome - pass				fail - learning outcome
Next bigger, better ideas to test from the start	P4	F4		Why didn't it work, and what to avoid
Changes or improvements for next level	P5	F5		Why didn't it work, but can be changed
What elements can be reused into other ideas	P6	F6		Why didn't it work, but a new better idea

learning   **What did you learn from whether a pass or a failure**
use the letter code and number your learning's

_____

_____

_____

_____

_____

_____

name	

description	
Short and simple description of the growth hack	

problem	
Short and specific description of the growth problem your solving	

results	measure	costs	ROI
# %	# %	low mid high	low mid high

timeframe

15 min	30 min	1 hour	1 day	2 days	3 days	4 days	5 days	7 days	10 days

Other time

HACK - *profile*

customer	
Who will by paying for this	

user	
Who will be consuming this	

middlemen	
Who is in the middle and why	

mindset

Knowledge needed to solve this sort of problem and how to go about it

skillset

The skills needed specifically to execute this growth hack

toolset

List all tools needed for execute this growth hack

HACK – *sequencing*

sequence   **Data / tools / conditions / sources / techniques / process**
Use the sequence numbers in your drawings as references below

_____

_____

_____

_____

_____

_____

_____

_____

_____

_____

_____

_____

_____

_____

HACK – *testing* **4**

pass				fail
Complete pass go to scale	P1	F1		Complete failure **discard**
Improve it to make better	P2	F2		**Modifications** to pass
Add on to it to make better	P3	F3		**New** idea to pass

learning outcome - pass				fail - learning outcome
Next bigger, better ideas to test from the start	P4	F4		Why didn't it work, and what to avoid
Changes or improvements for next level	P5	F5		Why didn't it work, but can be changed
What elements can be reused into other ideas	P6	F6		Why didn't it work, but a new better idea

learning — **What did you learn from whether a pass or a failure**
use the letter code and number your learning's

_____

_____

_____

_____

_____

_____

customer

Who will by
paying for this

user

Who will be
consuming this

middlemen

Who is in the
middle and why

mindset

Knowledge
needed to solve
this sort of
problem and how
to go about it

skillset

The skills needed
specifically to
execute this
growth hack

toolset

List all tools
needed for
execute this
growth hack

HACK – *sequencing*   **5**

sequence

Data / tools / conditions / sources / techniques / process
Use the sequence numbers in your drawings as references below

_____

_____

_____

_____

_____

_____

_____

_____

_____

_____

_____

_____

_____

_____

_____

_____

_____

5   **HACK** – *sequencing*

HACK - *testing* 5

pass				fail
Complete pass go to scale	P1	F1		Complete failure **discard**
Improve it to make better	P2	F2		**Modifications** to pass
Add on to it to make better	P3	F3		**New** idea to pass

learning outcome - pass				fail - learning outcome
Next bigger, better ideas to test from the start	P4	F4		Why didn't it work, and what to avoid
Changes or improvements for next level	P5	F5		Why didn't it work, but can be changed
What elements can be reused into other ideas	P6	F6		Why didn't it work, but a new better idea

learning — **What did you learn from whether a pass or a failure**
use the letter code and number your learning's

_____

_____

_____

_____

_____

_____

learning

big learning big ideas based
on the past 5 hacks

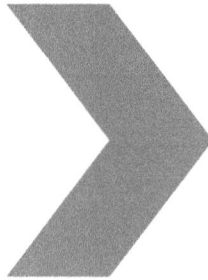

| 1 - 5 | 6 - 10 | 11 - 15 | 16 - 20 |

First quarter done – lets
capture those leanings

common

What did you find in common among the last few hacks
List them as raw observations

_____

_____

_____

_____

_____

_____

fails

Convert fails into new outcomes to explore
List them in order of importance

_____

_____

_____

_____

_____

_____

_____

HACK – *learning*

pass
Convert successes into new outcomes to explore
List them in order of importance

_____

_____

_____

_____

_____

_____

new hacks
Take major learning from pass/failed outcomes into new hacks
List them in order of importance

_____

_____

_____

_____

_____

_____

25%

complete

learning

*Go to **page 290** and capture all learning's*

Go to **page 290**

HACK – *profile*

name	

description	
Short and simple description of the growth hack	

problem	
Short and specific description of the growth problem your solving	

results		measure		costs			ROI		
#	%	#	%	low	mid	high	low	mid	high

timeframe

15 min	30 min	1 hour	1 day	2 days	3 days	4 days	5 days	7 days	10 days

Other time

Growth thinking   120

6   HACK - *profile*

customer

Who will by paying for this

user

Who will be consuming this

middlemen

Who is in the middle and why

mindset

Knowledge needed to solve this sort of problem and how to go about it

skillset

The skills needed specifically to execute this growth hack

toolset

List all tools needed for execute this growth hack

.

sequence   **Data / tools / conditions / sources / techniques / process**
Use the sequence numbers in your drawings as references below

6   **HACK** – *sequencing*

pass			**fail**
Complete pass go to scale	P1	F1	Complete failure **discard**
Improve it to make better	P2	F2	**Modifications** to pass
Add on to it to make better	P3	F3	**New** idea to pass

learning outcome - pass			**fail - learning outcome**
Next bigger, better ideas to test from the start	P4	F4	Why didn't it work, and what to avoid
Changes or improvements for next level	P5	F5	Why didn't it work, but can be changed
What elements can be reused into other ideas	P6	F6	Why didn't it work, but a new better idea

learning **What did you learn from whether a pass or a failure**
use the letter code and number your learning's

_____

_____

_____

_____

_____

_____

_____

HACK – *profile*

name	

description	
Short and simple description of the growth hack	

problem	
Short and specific description of the growth problem your solving	

results	measure	costs	ROI
# %	# %	low mid high	low mid high

timeframe									
15 min	30 min	1 hour	1 day	2 days	3 days	4 days	5 days	7 days	10 days

Other time

customer

Who will by paying for this

user

Who will be consuming this

middlemen

Who is in the middle and why

mindset

Knowledge needed to solve this sort of problem and how to go about it

skillset

The skills needed specifically to execute this growth hack

toolset

List all tools needed for execute this growth hack

HACK – *sequencing*

7

| sequence | **Data / tools / conditions / sources / techniques / process**
Use the sequence numbers in your drawings as references below |

_____

_____

_____

_____

_____

_____

_____

_____

_____

_____

_____

_____

_____

_____

_____

_____

	pass			fail	

Complete pass go to scale	P1	F1	Complete failure **discard**
Improve it to make better	P2	F2	**Modifications** to pass
Add on to it to make better	P3	F3	**New** idea to pass

learning outcome - pass		fail - learning outcome

Next bigger, better ideas to test from the start	P4	F4	Why didn't it work, and what to avoid
Changes or improvements for next level	P5	F5	Why didn't it work, but can be changed
What elements can be reused into other ideas	P6	F6	Why didn't it work, but a new better idea

learning **What did you learn from whether a pass or a failure**
use the letter code and number your learning's

_____

_____

_____

_____

_____

_____

HACK – *profile*

name	

description

Short and simple
description of the
growth hack

problem

Short and specific
description of the
growth problem
your solving

results		measure		costs			ROI		
#	%	#	%	low	mid	high	low	mid	high

timeframe

15 min	30 min	1 hour	1 day	2 days	3 days	4 days	5 days	7 days	10 days

Other time

customer

Who will by
paying for this

user

Who will be
consuming this

middlemen

Who is in the
middle and why

mindset

Knowledge
needed to solve
this sort of
problem and how
to go about it

skillset

The skills needed
specifically to
execute this
growth hack

toolset

List all tools
needed   for
execute this
growth hack

HACK – *sequencing*

8

sequence

Data / tools / conditions / sources / techniques / process
Use the sequence numbers in your drawings as references below

_____

_____

_____

_____

_____

_____

_____

_____

_____

_____

_____

_____

_____

_____

_____

HACK – *testing*

	pass			fail	

Complete pass go to scale	P1	F1	Complete failure **discard**
Improve it to make better	P2	F2	**Modifications** to pass
Add on to it to make better	P3	F3	**New** idea to pass

learning outcome - pass | | | **fail - learning outcome**

Next bigger, better ideas to test from the start	P4	F4	Why didn't it work, and what to avoid
Changes or improvements for next level	P5	F5	Why didn't it work, but can be changed
What elements can be reused into other ideas	P6	F6	Why didn't it work, but a new better idea

learning **What did you learn from whether a pass or a failure**
use the letter code and number your learning's

_____

_____

_____

_____

_____

_____

HACK – *profile*

name

description

Short and simple description of the growth hack

problem

Short and specific description of the growth problem your solving

results		measure		costs			ROI		
#	%	#	%	low	mid	high	low	mid	high

timeframe

15 min	30 min	1 hour	1 day	2 days	3 days	4 days	5 days	7 days	10 days

Other time

9

HACK - *profile*

customer	
Who will by paying for this	

user	
Who will be consuming this	

middlemen	
Who is in the middle and why	

mindset

Knowledge needed to solve this sort of problem and how to go about it

skillset

The skills needed specifically to execute this growth hack

toolset

List all tools needed for execute this growth hack

Hack

sequence

Data / tools / conditions / sources / techniques / process
Use the sequence numbers in your drawings as references below

pass				fail
Complete pass go to scale	P1	F1		Complete failure **discard**
Improve it to make better	P2	F2		**Modifications** to pass
Add on to it to make better	P3	F3		**New** idea to pass

learning outcome - pass			fail - learning outcome
Next bigger, better ideas to test from the start	P4	F4	Why didn't it work, and what to avoid
Changes or improvements for next level	P5	F5	Why didn't it work, but can be changed
What elements can be reused into other ideas	P6	F6	Why didn't it work, but a new better idea

learning

What did you learn from whether a pass or a failure
use the letter code and number your learning's

_____

_____

_____

_____

_____

_____

_____

_____

_____

_____

_____

_____

_____

_____

_____

_____

_____

_____

_____

_____

_____

name	

description	
Short and simple description of the growth hack	

problem	
Short and specific description of the growth problem your solving	

results		measure		costs			ROI		
#	%	#	%	low	mid	high	low	mid	high

timeframe

15 min	30 min	1 hour	1 day	2 days	3 days	4 days	5 days	7 days	10 days

Other time

customer

Who will by
paying for this

user

Who will be
consuming this

middlemen

Who is in the
middle and why

mindset

Knowledge
needed to solve
this sort of
problem and how
to go about it

skillset

The skills needed
specifically to
execute this
growth hack

toolset

List all tools
needed for
execute this
growth hack

HACK – *sequencing*

10

| sequence | **Data / tools / conditions / sources / techniques / process**
Use the sequence numbers in your drawings as references below |

	pass			fail	
Complete pass go to scale	P1		F1	Complete failure **discard**	
Improve it to make better	P2		F2	**Modifications** to pass	
Add on to it to make better	P3		F3	**New** idea to pass	

learning outcome - pass			fail - learning outcome	
Next bigger, better ideas to test from the start	P4	F4	Why didn't it work, and what to avoid	
Changes or improvements for next level	P5	F5	Why didn't it work, but can be changed	
What elements can be reused into other ideas	P6	F6	Why didn't it work, but a new better idea	

learning	**What did you learn from whether a pass or a failure**
	use the letter code and number your learning's

_____

_____

_____

_____

_____

_____

learning

big learning big ideas based
on the past 5 hacks

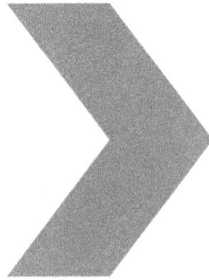

1 - 5   6 - 10   11 - 15   16 - 20

Second quarter done – lets
capture those leanings

common	**What did you find in common among the last few hacks**
	List them as raw observations

_____

_____

_____

_____

_____

fails	**Convert fails into new outcomes to explore**
	List them in order of importance

_____

_____

_____

_____

_____

_____

_____

HACK – *learning*

pass | **Convert successes into new outcomes to explore**
List them in order of importance

_____

_____

_____

_____

_____

_____

new hacks | **Take major learning from pass/failed outcomes into new hacks**
List them in order of importance

_____

_____

_____

_____

_____

_____

_____

50%

complete

learning

*Go to **page 291** and capture all learning's*

Go to **page 291** and capture all learning's

HACK – *profile*

name	

description

Short and simple
description of the
growth hack

problem

Short and specific
description of the
growth problem
your solving

results		measure		costs			ROI		
#	%	#	%	low	mid	high	low	mid	high

timeframe

15 min	30 min	1 hour	1 day	2 days	3 days	4 days	5 days	7 days	10 days

Other time

customer	
Who will by paying for this	

user	
Who will be consuming this	

middlemen	
Who is in the middle and why	

mindset	
Knowledge needed to solve this sort of problem and how to go about it	

skillset	
The skills needed specifically to execute this growth hack	

toolset	
List all tools needed for execute this growth hack	

HACK – *sequencing*

sequence **Data / tools / conditions / sources / techniques / process**
Use the sequence numbers in your drawings as references below

_____

_____

_____

_____

_____

_____

_____

_____

_____

_____

_____

_____

_____

_____

_____

HACK – *testing*

pass				fail
Complete pass go to scale	P1	F1		Complete failure **discard**
Improve it to make better	P2	F2		**Modifications** to pass
Add on to it to make better	P3	F3		**New** idea to pass

learning outcome - pass				fail - learning outcome
Next bigger, better ideas to test from the start	P4	F4		Why didn't it work, and what to avoid
Changes or improvements for next level	P5	F5		Why didn't it work, but can be changed
What elements can be reused into other ideas	P6	F6		Why didn't it work, but a new better idea

learning — **What did you learn from whether a pass or a failure**
use the letter code and number your learning's

_____

_____

_____

_____

_____

_____

name	

description

Short and simple
description of the
growth hack

problem

Short and specific
description of the
growth problem
your solving

results	measure	costs	ROI
# %	# %	low mid high	low mid high

timeframe

15 min	30 min	1 hour	1 day	2 days	3 days	4 days	5 days	7 days	10 days

Other time

customer

Who will by
paying for this

user

Who will be
consuming this

middlemen

Who is in the
middle and why

mindset

Knowledge
needed to solve
this sort of
problem and how
to go about it

skillset

The skills needed
specifically to
execute this
growth hack

toolset

List all tools
needed   for
execute this
growth hack

HACK – *sequencing*

sequence **Data / tools / conditions / sources / techniques / process**
Use the sequence numbers in your drawings as references below

HACK – *testing*

12

pass			**fail**
Complete pass go to scale	P1	F1	Complete failure **discard**
Improve it to make better	P2	F2	**Modifications** to pass
Add on to it to make better	P3	F3	**New** idea to pass

learning outcome - pass			**fail - learning outcome**
Next bigger, better ideas to test from the start	P4	F4	Why didn't it work, and what to avoid
Changes or improvements for next level	P5	F5	Why didn't it work, but can be changed
What elements can be reused into other ideas	P6	F6	Why didn't it work, but a new better idea

learning **What did you learn from whether a pass or a failure**
use the letter code and number your learning's

_____

_____

_____

_____

_____

_____

_____

_____

_____

_____

_____

_____

_____

_____

_____

_____

_____

_____

_____

_____

_____

HACK – *profile*

13

name	

description

Short and simple description of the growth hack

problem

Short and specific description of the growth problem your solving

results	measure	costs	ROI
# %	# %	low mid high	low mid high

timeframe

15 min	30 min	1 hour	1 day	2 days	3 days	4 days	5 days	7 days	10 days

Other time

customer

Who will by
paying for this

user

Who will be
consuming this

middlemen

Who is in the
middle and why

mindset

Knowledge
needed to solve
this sort of
problem and how
to go about it

skillset

The skills needed
specifically to
execute this
growth hack

toolset

List all tools
needed for
execute this
growth hack

HACK – *sequencing*

13

sequence **Data / tools / conditions / sources / techniques / process**
Use the sequence numbers in your drawings as references below

_____

_____

_____

_____

_____

_____

_____

_____

_____

_____

_____

_____

_____

_____

_____

_____

HACK - *testing*

13

pass			**fail**	
Complete pass go to scale	P1	F1	Complete failure **discard**
Improve it to make better	P2	F2	**Modifications** to pass
Add on to it to make better	P3	F3	**New** idea to pass

learning outcome - pass			**fail - learning outcome**	
Next bigger, better ideas to test from the start	P4	F4	Why didn't it work, and what to avoid
Changes or improvements for next level	P5	F5	Why didn't it work, but can be changed
What elements can be reused into other ideas	P6	F6	Why didn't it work, but a new better idea

learning **What did you learn from whether a pass or a failure**
use the letter code and number your learning's

_____

_____

_____

_____

_____

_____

HACK – *profile* 14

name	

description
Short and simple description of the growth hack

problem
Short and specific description of the growth problem your solving

results	measure	costs	ROI
# %	# %	low mid high	low mid high

timeframe

15 min	30 min	1 hour	1 day	2 days	3 days	4 days	5 days	7 days	10 days

Other time

HACK - *profile*

customer

Who will by
paying for this

user

Who will be
consuming this

middlemen

Who is in the
middle and why

mindset

Knowledge
needed to solve
this sort of
problem and how
to go about it

skillset

The skills needed
specifically to
execute this
growth hack

toolset

List all tools
needed for
execute this
growth hack

HACK – *sequencing*

14

sequence

Data / tools / conditions / sources / techniques / process
Use the sequence numbers in your drawings as references below

---

---

pass			fail
Complete pass go to scale	P1	F1	Complete failure **discard**
Improve it to make better	P2	F2	**Modifications** to pass
Add on to it to make better	P3	F3	**New** idea to pass

learning outcome - pass			fail - learning outcome
Next bigger, better ideas to test from the start	P4	F4	Why didn't it work, and what to avoid
Changes or improvements for next level	P5	F5	Why didn't it work, but can be changed
What elements can be reused into other ideas	P6	F6	Why didn't it work, but a new better idea

learning   **What did you learn from whether a pass or a failure**
use the letter code and number your learning's

_____

_____

_____

_____

_____

_____

name	

description

Short and simple description of the growth hack

problem

Short and specific description of the growth problem your solving

results		measure		costs			ROI		
#	%	#	%	low	mid	high	low	mid	high

timeframe

15 min	30 min	1 hour	1 day	2 days	3 days	4 days	5 days	7 days	10 days

Other time

15   **HACK** - *profile*

customer	
Who will by paying for this	

user	
Who will be consuming this	

middlemen	
Who is in the middle and why	

mindset

Knowledge needed to solve this sort of problem and how to go about it

skillset

The skills needed specifically to execute this growth hack

toolset

List all tools needed for execute this growth hack

HACK – *sequencing*   **15**

sequence   **Data / tools / conditions / sources / techniques / process**
Use the sequence numbers in your drawings as references below

_____

_____

_____

_____

_____

_____

_____

_____

_____

_____

_____

_____

_____

_____

_____

_____

pass			fail
Complete pass go to scale	P1	F1	Complete failure **discard**
Improve it to make better	P2	F2	**Modifications** to pass
Add on to it to make better	P3	F3	**New** idea to pass

learning outcome - pass			fail - learning outcome
Next bigger, better ideas to test from the start	P4	F4	Why didn't it work, and what to avoid
Changes or improvements for next level	P5	F5	Why didn't it work, but can be changed
What elements can be reused into other ideas	P6	F6	Why didn't it work, but a new better idea

learning

What did you learn from whether a pass or a failure
use the letter code and number your learning's

_____

_____

_____

_____

_____

_____

_____

_____

_____

_____

_____

_____

_____

_____

_____

_____

_____

_____

_____

_____

_____

_____

learning

big learning big ideas based
on the past 5 hacks

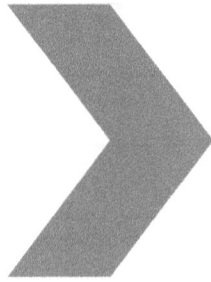

1 - 5   6 - 10   11 - 15   **16 - 20**

Third quarter done – lets
capture those leanings

common — **What did you find in common among the last few hacks**
List them as raw observations

_____

_____

_____

_____

_____

_____

fails — **Convert fails into new outcomes to explore**
List them in order of importance

_____

_____

_____

_____

_____

_____

HACK – *learning*

pass **Convert successes into new outcomes to explore**
List them in order of importance

_____

_____

_____

_____

_____

_____

new hacks **Take major learning from pass/failed outcomes into new hacks**
List them in order of importance

_____

_____

_____

_____

_____

_____

_____

75%

complete

learning

*Go to **page 292** and capture all learning's*

name	

description

Short and simple
description of the
growth hack

problem

Short and specific
description of the
growth problem
your solving

results	measure	costs	ROI
# %	# %	low mid high	low mid high

timeframe

15 min	30 min	1 hour	1 day	2 days	3 days	4 days	5 days	7 days	10 days

Other time

customer

Who will by
paying for this

user

Who will be
consuming this

middlemen

Who is in the
middle and why

mindset

Knowledge
needed to solve
this sort of
problem and how
to go about it

skillset

The skills needed
specifically to
execute this
growth hack

toolset

List all tools
needed for
execute this
growth hack

HACK – *sequencing*

sequence | **Data / tools / conditions / sources / techniques / process**
Use the sequence numbers in your drawings as references below

_____

_____

_____

_____

_____

_____

_____

_____

_____

_____

_____

_____

_____

_____

HACK – *testing*

16

pass			fail
Complete pass go to scale	P1	F1	Complete failure **discard**
Improve it to make better	P2	F2	**Modifications** to pass
Add on to it to make better	P3	F3	**New** idea to pass

learning outcome - pass			fail - learning outcome
Next bigger, better ideas to test from the start	P4	F4	Why didn't it work, and what to avoid
Changes or improvements for next level	P5	F5	Why didn't it work, but can be changed
What elements can be reused into other ideas	P6	F6	Why didn't it work, but a new better idea

learning **What did you learn from whether a pass or a failure**
use the letter code and number your learning's

_____

_____

_____

_____

_____

_____

HACK – *profile*

17

name	

description

Short and simple
description of the
growth hack

problem

Short and specific
description of the
growth problem
your solving

results		measure		costs			ROI		
#	%	#	%	low	mid	high	low	mid	high

timeframe

15 min	30 min	1 hour	1 day	2 days	3 days	4 days	5 days	7 days	10 days

Other time

customer

Who will by
paying for this

user

Who will be
consuming this

middlemen

Who is in the
middle and why

mindset

Knowledge
needed to solve
this sort of
problem and how
to go about it

skillset

The skills needed
specifically to
execute this
growth hack

toolset

List all tools
needed for
execute this
growth hack

| sequence | **Data / tools / conditions / sources / techniques / process**
Use the sequence numbers in your drawings as references below |

_____

_____

_____

_____

_____

_____

_____

_____

_____

_____

_____

_____

_____

_____

_____

_____

pass				fail
Complete pass go to scale	P1	F1		Complete failure **discard**
Improve it to make better	P2	F2		**Modifications** to pass
Add on to it to make better	P3	F3		**New** idea to pass

learning outcome - pass				fail - learning outcome
Next bigger, better ideas to test from the start	P4	F4		Why didn't it work, and what to avoid
Changes or improvements for next level	P5	F5		Why didn't it work, but can be changed
What elements can be reused into other ideas	P6	F6		Why didn't it work, but a new better idea

learning   **What did you learn from whether a pass or a failure**
use the letter code and number your learning's

_____

_____

_____

_____

_____

_____

name	

description

Short and simple
description of the
growth hack

problem

Short and specific
description of the
growth problem
your solving

results		measure		costs			ROI		
#	%	#	%	low	mid	high	low	mid	high

timeframe

15 min	30 min	1 hour	1 day	2 days	3 days	4 days	5 days	7 days	10 days

Other time

customer

Who will by paying for this

user

Who will be consuming this

middlemen

Who is in the middle and why

mindset

Knowledge needed to solve this sort of problem and how to go about it

skillset

The skills needed specifically to execute this growth hack

toolset

List all tools needed for execute this growth hack

HACK – *sequencing* 18

sequence **Data / tools / conditions / sources / techniques / process**
Use the sequence numbers in your drawings as references below

_____

_____

_____

_____

_____

_____

_____

_____

_____

_____

_____

_____

_____

_____

_____

pass			**fail**
Complete pass go to scale	P1	F1	Complete failure **discard**
Improve it to make better	P2	F2	**Modifications** to pass
Add on to it to make better	P3	F3	**New** idea to pass

learning outcome - pass			**fail - learning outcome**
Next bigger, better ideas to test from the start	P4	F4	Why didn't it work, and what to avoid
Changes or improvements for next level	P5	F5	Why didn't it work, but can be changed
What elements can be reused into other ideas	P6	F6	Why didn't it work, but a new better idea

learning   **What did you learn from whether a pass or a failure**
use the letter code and number your learning's

_____

_____

_____

_____

_____

_____

name	

description

Short and simple
description of the
growth hack

problem

Short and specific
description of the
growth problem
your solving

results	measure	costs	ROI
# %	# %	low mid high	low mid high

timeframe

15 min	30 min	1 hour	1 day	2 days	3 days	4 days	5 days	7 days	10 days

Other time

HACK - *profile*

customer
Who will by
paying for this

user
Who will be
consuming this

middlemen
Who is in the
middle and why

mindset
Knowledge
needed to solve
this sort of
problem and how
to go about it

skillset
The skills needed
specifically to
execute this
growth hack

toolset
List all tools
needed for
execute this
growth hack

HACK – *sequencing* **19**

| sequence | **Data / tools / conditions / sources / techniques / process**
Use the sequence numbers in your drawings as references below |

_____

_____

_____

_____

_____

_____

_____

_____

_____

_____

_____

_____

_____

_____

_____

_____

HACK – *testing*

19

	pass			fail	
Complete pass go to scale	P1		F1	Complete failure **discard**	
Improve it to make better	P2		F2	**Modifications** to pass	
Add on to it to make better	P3		F3	**New** idea to pass	

	learning outcome - pass			fail - learning outcome	
Next bigger, better ideas to test from the start	P4		F4	Why didn't it work, and what to avoid	
Changes or improvements for next level	P5		F5	Why didn't it work, but can be changed	
What elements can be reused into other ideas	P6		F6	Why didn't it work, but a new better idea	

learning	**What did you learn from whether a pass or a failure** *use the letter code and number your learning's*

_____

_____

_____

_____

_____

_____

HACK – *profile*

name	

description

Short and simple description of the growth hack

problem

Short and specific description of the growth problem your solving

results		measure		costs			ROI		
#	%	#	%	low	mid	high	low	mid	high

timeframe

15 min	30 min	1 hour	1 day	2 days	3 days	4 days	5 days	7 days	10 days

Other time

20

HACK - *profile*

customer	
Who will by paying for this	

user	
Who will be consuming this	

middlemen	
Who is in the middle and why	

mindset

Knowledge needed to solve this sort of problem and how to go about it

skillset

The skills needed specifically to execute this growth hack

toolset

List all tools needed for execute this growth hack

HACK - *sequencing*   **20**

sequence   **Data / tools / conditions / sources / techniques / process**
Use the sequence numbers in your drawings as references below

---

HACK - *testing*   **20**

pass				fail
Complete pass go to scale	P1	F1		Complete failure **discard**
Improve it to make better	P2	F2		**Modifications** to pass
Add on to it to make better	P3	F3		**New** idea to pass

learning outcome - pass				fail - learning outcome
Next bigger, better ideas to test from the start	P4	F4		Why didn't it work, and what to avoid
Changes or improvements for next level	P5	F5		Why didn't it work, but can be changed
What elements can be reused into other ideas	P6	F6		Why didn't it work, but a new better idea

learning   **What did you learn from whether a pass or a failure**
use the letter code and number your learning's

_____

_____

_____

_____

_____

_____

learning

big learning big ideas based
on the past 5 hacks

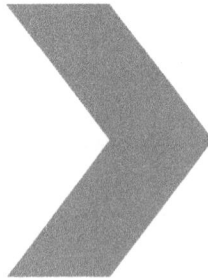

| 1 - 5 | 6 - 10 | 11 - 15 | 16 - 20 |

Fourth quarter done – lets
capture those leanings

HACK *– learning*

common   **What did you find in common among the last few hacks**
List them as raw observations

_____

_____

_____

_____

_____

_____

fails   **Convert fails into new outcomes to explore**
List them in order of importance

_____

_____

_____

_____

_____

_____

_____

pass   **Convert successes into new outcomes to explore**
List them in order of importance

_____

_____

_____

_____

_____

_____

new hacks   **Take major learning from pass/failed outcomes into new hacks**
List them in order of importance

_____

_____

_____

_____

_____

_____

Complete – 100%

learning

*Go to **page 293** and capture all learning's*

LEARNING

converting leanings into
new growth hacks

LEARNING

LEARNING

new hacks   **Take major learning from pass/failed outcomes into new hacks**
List them in order of importance

_____

_____

_____

_____

_____

_____

_____

_____

_____

_____

_____

_____

_____

■■■■■■ ☐☐☐☐☐ ☐☐☐☐☐ ☐☐☐☐☐

new hacks | **Take major learning from pass/failed outcomes into new hacks**
List them in order of importance

new hacks **Take major learning from pass/failed outcomes into new hacks**
List them in order of importance

LEARNING

new hacks **Take major learning from pass/failed outcomes into new hacks**
List them in order of importance

_____

_____

_____

_____

_____

_____

_____

_____

_____

_____

_____

_____

_____

LEARNING

next hacks **What are your next big hacks**
List them in order of importance

- [ ]
- [ ]
- [ ]
- [ ]
- [ ]
- [ ]
- [ ]

ABOUT THE AUTHOR

Nader Sabry is a keynote speaker, strategist, innovator, and entrepreneur as well as a leading voice in innovation, space technology, government, and health/wellness. He is a passionate advocate for inspiring the youth to embrace science and technology, through the Get2space.com initiative in partnership with the US Space Foundation.

Sabry has directly raised US $20 million in venture capital, indirectly $100 million for startups he has advised or cofounded, and $3 billion in foreign direct investment. He was the 43rd person in history to be NASA Space Technology certified, has served as a judge for the US Space Foundation's Space Technology Hall of Fame, is a top-50 writer globally on medium.com, has been ranked one of the top 13 innovators in the MENA region making a difference by Step Conference, and was featured by A.T. Kearney as one of their top alumni.

Sabry is the former CEO and Founder of TIMEZ5 Global Inc.; a Canadian space technology certified company by NASA's Space Foundation, and a GIES Innovation award winner from His Highness Sheikh Mohammed Bin Rashid Al Maktoum. TIMEZ5 was founded 2012 after five years of R&D selling in 37 countries; it has been recommended by healthcare professionals globally.

Prior to TIMEZ5 Global, Sabry was head of innovation and thought leadership at A.T. Kearney, chief strategist for The Dubai Department of Economic Development, and director of strategy for the Dubai Foreign Investment Office. He has also advised several governments and Fortune 1000 companies.

ABOUT THE AUTHOR

Sabry contributes to innovation globally as a published author, speaker, and lecturer, and as the former chairman of the Institute for Strategy Complexity Management forum. Additionally, he has been featured in Time Magazine, Huffington Post, Financial times – merger markets, MIT Technology Review, and NASA's premier publication Spin-off.

As a University of Cambridge graduate, Sabry attained his postgraduate education in business administration and holds an MBA, BComm, and business diploma.

Sabry's work has been described as,
"He is the guy you don't want your competition to hire...."

SCAN & START NOW

Scan this QR code and get **FREE training** on how to effectible use the growth Thinking methodology
$298 in value for free

Quickly learn how to use the Growth thinking methodology **like a Ninja**

+ *$99 hacking* growth thinking designs training **course FREE**

+ *$199* **10 secrets** of Growth Thinking training ***course FREE*** www.My**Growth**Thinking.com